Verbal Reasoning Test by Rian Crombie.

ISBN: 9781720056966
Imprint: Independently published

THE TEST

The verbal reasoning test is designed to test your verbal comprehension ability, ensuring that it is adequate to carry out the day to day duties of a Police Officer or PCSO.

Each test consists of 5 questions with multiple choice answers. The difficulty of the questions varies from challenging to fairly simple. Some questions need a good understanding of the facts, therefore it is important to thoroughly read through each question.

You will have 12 minutes to complete the 5 questions. The 12-minute limit is designed to add pressure, but remember to remain calm and work through each question logically, accurately and as quickly as possible. If you aim to spend approximately 2 minutes on each question, you should be able to finish nearly all the questions.

HOW TO PREPARE

The verbal reasoning test examines your verbal skills and comprehension. As with any other test or exam it is important to thoroughly prepare; this involves learning or re-learning your basic reasoning skills.

The tests in this guide will help you to brush-up on your skills so that you will eventually be able to pass the test with relative ease.

This, coupled with extensive revision and practice using internet and book resources, will help you become more confident and accurate in the test.

TEST PAPER 1   12 MINS

On the evening of December 21 Peterborough Boat Club was vandalised. The police are carrying out investigations.

The only facts known at this stage are:

• The boat club insurance had lapsed.
• The club Chairman was Nick Foster.
• Gary Newman owns a boat at the club.
• Gary Newman had fallen out with Nick Foster.
• Gary Newman was away on Holiday the week before Christmas.
• No boats were damaged.
• The Club house keys were found in Gary Newman's house.

A = TRUE B = FALSE C = IMPOSSIBLE TO SAY

1. Nick Foster may have vandalised the boat club.
2. The Club will be able to claim on their insurance.
3. Gary Newman visited the boat club on December 21.
4. Nick Foster could have been at the boat club when the vandalism took place.
5. There are definite grounds to arrest Gary Newman for vandalism.

TEST PAPER 2   12 MINS

On July 28, the gym at King Edward Grammar School, in Smithfield, was burnt to the ground. Only the local Fire and Rescue service attended the scene at 21:00.

The only facts known at this stage are:

• A local teenager, John Hallam, was at the school at 20:00.
• John Hallam was expelled from school a fortnight ago for bad behaviour.
• The gym alarm was on.
• The fire was started using a petrol bomb.
• The ambulance service attended the scene at 21:30.
• A King Edward Grammar School pupil, Sally Jones, was admitted to hospital on July 28.

A = TRUE B = FALSE C = IMPOSSIBLE TO SAY

1. The Police and Fire and Rescue service attended the scene at 21:00.
2. John Hallam may have petrol bombed the gym.
3. John Hallam was expelled from King Edward Grammar School.
4. Sally Jones was injured in the fire.
5. The gym alarm may not have sounded when set off.

TEST PAPER 3   12 MINS

Tony Murphy was stabbed on the evening of October 17 in Upton Park, Sudbury. He later died in hospital from his injuries.

The only facts known at this stage are:

• He was stabbed in the heart
• Tony left a local pub near Upton Park at 7pm.
• A dead body was found in the Upton Park area at 10pm.
• Tony had visited a cash machine before entering the park.
• Tony was heavily drunk.
• Tony left his home for the pub at 2pm.

A = TRUE B = FALSE C = IMPOSSIBLE TO SAY

1. Tony was drinking alcohol for 5 hours.
2. Tony's dead body was found in the park at 22:00hrs.
3. Tony may have been robbed and stabbed for money.
4. Tony was knifed in the heart.
5. Tony died from his injuries at the scene.

TEST PAPER 4   12 MINS

After 12-years of marriage, Jane Smith left her husband Tom Smith and moved to a different town.

The only facts known at this stage are:

• Tom cheated on Jane during their marriage.
• Jane wanted to move to Driffield.
• Jane and Tom have been divorced for two-years.
• Tom has a new partner called Sarah.
• Tom and Jane got married when they were twenty two.
• Tom and Sarah have a three-year-old child together.

A = TRUE B = FALSE C = IMPOSSIBLE TO SAY

1. Jane was 36 years old when she and Tom got divorced.
2. Tom and Jane have a three-year-old child together.
3. Tom slept with Sarah while he was still married to Jane.
4. Toms philandering was the reason for the divorce.
5. Jane left Tom and moved to Driffield.

On July 5 at 15:10 a light aircraft crash-landed in a field. There were two people inside the plane - one died from his injuries. The killed crash victim was identified as Ken Stone, an aviation enthusiast, from Retford.

The only facts known at this stage are:

• The aircraft took off from a local airfield at 2pm.
• An increase in bird activity was reported in the area surrounding the airfield.
• The nearest airfield to Retford is Gamston.
• A mayday call was heard at 15:05.
• Ken Stone visited the Gamston airfield every weekend.
• The crash occurred two-miles south of Waddington Airfield.

A = TRUE B = FALSE C = IMPOSSIBLE TO SAY

1. Ken Stone was the pilot of the light aircraft.
2. The plane may have had a bird strike leading the crash.
3. The emergency occurred at 15:05.
4. The light aircraft was in the air for one-hour 20-minutes before it crashed.
5. The aircraft took off from Waddington Airfield.

A 53-year-old man was found dead near a lake by his car. A post mortem examination was carried out on the body and it was found that the man died from a gunshot wound to his head.

The only facts known at this stage are:

- Melvin Jones' only daughter recently died in a car accident.
- Melvin Jones had life insurance worth £600,000.
- The man in the car was identified as Melvin Jones.
- Melvin Jones took the death of his daughter very badly.
- Caroline planned to divorce her husband.

A = TRUE B = FALSE C = IMPOSSIBLE TO SAY

1. Melvin Jones might have committed suicide.
2. Melvin Jones was murdered.
3. Melvin Jones could not face life without his daughter.
4. Caroline planned to kill Melvin for the insurance money.
5. Melvin has had only one child.

A lorry depot was broken into between 11:00pm and 04:00am. The night guard was on duty between 09:00pm and 03:00am. It was discovered that the depot had been broken into at 04:00am. A window was found broken on the south side of the building.

The only facts known at this stage are:

• The night guard reported no problems while on duty.
• A local resident saw a man acting suspiciously around the depot at 12:15pm.
• The depot stored high priced electronics.
• The depot had repeatedly reported lost stock items.
• The robbery occurred on Saturday morning.
• There was no CCTV evidence.

A = TRUE B = FALSE C = IMPOSSIBLE TO SAY

1. A suspicious woman was seen around the depot at 12:15pm.
2. The thief broke in through a window on the north side of the building.
3. The break in occurred between 03:00 am and 04:00 am on Saturday.
4. The CCTV evidence may have been removed from the depot.
5. Windows may be broken on the north side of the building.

TEST PAPER 8   12 MINS

At 01:45am door staff ejected two drunken men from a nightclub. At 02:30am two members of door staff were seriously assaulted, resulting in both of them being admitted to hospital. One man is in a stable condition while the other is in a critical condition, undergoing immediate surgery. These were the only door staff admitted to the hospital during the early hours of the morning.

The only facts known at this stage are:

• Door staff ejected Ben Shamrock and Rob Holmes from a nightclub.
• Ben Shamrock had previous convictions for assault.
• Dave Meadows was admitted to hospital with a stab wound to his chest.
• Dave Meadows and Tim Smith work for Wildcat nightclub as doormen.
• Ben Shamrock stabbed Dave Meadows in the chest.
• Tim Smith was admitted to hospital following an assault- he remains in a stable condition.
• Tim Smith only works on a Friday night.

A = TRUE B = FALSE C = IMPOSSIBLE TO SAY

1. Ben Shamrock stabbed Dave Meadows in the chest.
2. Dave Meadows had to undergo immediate surgery.
3. The assault occurred outside Wildcat nightclub.
4. Ben Shamrock and Rob Holmes were ejected from the Wildcat nightclub prior to the
offence.
5. The assault occurred on a Saturday night at 02:30 am.

On Sunday, December 7, Police Traffic Officers attended a fatal road traffic incident. The Police were at the scene of the incident from 2:10am. There were two male passengers and one female passenger in a car. There was one fatality in the collision.

The only facts known at this stage are:

• Jamie Matlock is the owner of the vehicle.
• Jamie was out drinking in a nightclub from 21:00 Saturday until 02:00 Sunday.
• Jamie has a girlfriend called Karen Miller.
• A female from the accident was pronounced dead at hospital.
• Jamie's best friend Tom Anderson has previous drink driving convictions.
• The driver of the vehicle was not insured.
• No pedestrians were involved.

A = TRUE B = FALSE C = IMPOSSIBLE TO SAY

1. Jamie Matlock was the driver of the vehicle.
2. A pedestrian may have been killed.
3. Karen Miller died in the accident.
4. Jamie drove his vehicle to the nightclub at 21:30.
5. Tom Anderson was driving the vehicle under the influence of alcohol.

TEST PAPER 10   12 MINS

On Saturday, May 7, a school caretaker found a number of broken windows on the northside of the school building. A local teenager was seen on a CCTV camera loitering in the vicinity of the school. He was recorded later leaving the area. He was identified as Graham Smyth.

The only facts known at this stage are:

• Graham Smyth once attended Melton Grammar School.
• The caretaker works from 08:00 until 14:00 on a Saturday.
• There were no broken windows when the caretaker locked up on Friday evening at18:00.
• Local teenagers play golf on the pitches towards the north of the school.
• Graham Smyth had recently been expelled from The Melton School.
• The school only has CCTV on the south side of the building.
• The caretaker works for Melton Grammar School.

A = TRUE B = FALSE C = IMPOSSIBLE TO SAY

1. The windows were broken between the hours of 18:00 Friday and 08:00 Saturday.
2. Graham Smyth may have broken the windows in a revenge attack for being expelled from the school.
3. CCTV could have recorded the windows being broken.
4. Golf balls could have broken the windows.
5. Graham Smyth was playing golf.

TEST PAPER 11   12 MINS

The Southton Police Incident Response Team (IRT) was called to a domestic violence incident on a Saturday evening at approximately 22:00. On arrival they discovered a female who had been seriously assaulted. A male was arrested and later charged with assault. His mother, the homeowner, called the police.

The only facts known at this stage are:

• The victim had repeatedly been assaulted by her brother Ross Jones.
• The Police IRT consists of two officers.
• Police attended one domestic violence call on Saturday night at 2 Clermont Drive.
• Katherine Jones is the owner of 2 Clermont Drive.
• Katherine Jones' daughter Sara Dolby was staying over that night.

A = TRUE B = FALSE C = IMPOSSIBLE TO SAY

1. Ross Jones assaulted the female on Saturday night.
2. The assault happened on Saturday at 22:00.
3. Katherine Jones was the female assaulted.
4. A single Police Officer attended the scene.
5. Katherine Jones called the Police on Saturday at 10:00am.

TEST PAPER 12   12 MINS

A young child disappeared from a local food shop in Kinston after her mother became distracted at the counter. The mother asked the shop assistant to ring Kinston Police when she discovered her child had disappeared. The police arrived 10-minutes after they were called. Another shopper reported seeing the child being walked away from the shop by a male who was approximately 6-ft tall, with brown hair.

The only facts known at this stage are:

• The mother Miss Jenkins has red hair.
• Police were called at 10:25am on Saturday morning.
• Miss Jenkins had just spoken to her child's father 10-minutes prior to her disappearance.
• The child's name is Molly.
• Molly's father has brown hair and is approximately 5 ft 11.
• Tony Woods has a child with Miss Jenkins.

A = TRUE B = FALSE C = IMPOSSIBLE TO SAY

1. The Police arrived on the scene at 10.25am Saturday morning.
2. Tony Woods is Molly's father.
3. Molly's father may have taken her.
4. Molly disappeared from a food shop in Kinston.
5. Molly must have red or brown hair.

During the summer Mrs Olds called Neslington County Council on 12 occasions reporting anti-social behaviour. Twenty-five-per-cent of the calls were about local drunk Andy Young loitering and discarding empty beer cans in her garden. Half of all the calls were because local teenagers were causing a nuisance around her semi-detached house, including disturbing behaviour and criminal damage. Mrs Olds reported that she felt scared in her own home.

The only facts known at this stage are:

- Local teenagers have been stopped by police and found with alcohol near Mrs Olds property.
- Two calls were because next door neighbours were playing music too loud.
- The Ford family live next door to Mr and Mrs Olds.
- Mrs Olds' husband is retired.
- Mrs Olds lives next to a park were teenager frequent.
- A neighbour, Mr Cook, has been warned about playing music too loud

A = TRUE B = FALSE C = IMPOSSIBLE TO SAY

1. Mrs Olds called the council three times about Andy Young.
2. Mrs Olds is retired.
3. Mrs Olds reported Mr Cook twice for playing his music too loud.
4. The park is possibly a reason the anti-social behaviour occurs.
5. Alcohol is the main cause of the anti-social behaviour.

TEST PAPER 14   12 MINS

A kebab shop in Shrewsbury has had bricks and rocks thrown at its windows and doors on more than five separate occasions. The owner believes it to be race-related and has told the police that he thinks the latest incident was a local teenager called Louise Murphy. The incidents always occur between 22:00 and 24:00.

The only facts known at this stage are:

• Police know that Louis Murphy is subject to a tagging order.
• The owner of the shop is Malik Ahkmed.
• Louis cannot leave his house between the hours of 19:00 and 07:00.
• Malik Ahkmed has recently had an argument with another local kebab shop owner Stelios Romis.
• Stelios Romis employs a 17-year-girl old called Louise.
• Louise had prevsiously worked for Malik.
• The Police have only received three reports of windows and doors being broken by rocks and bricks being thrown at Malik's kebab shop (The Kebab House).

A = TRUE B = FALSE C = IMPOSSIBLE TO SAY

1. Malik's kebab shop's windows have been smashed repeatedly.
2. Louis Murphy may have thrown the bricks through the window.
3. Bricks and rocks were the only objects thrown.
4. Malik and Stelios had an argument about Louise.
5. Police were called after every incident.

TEST PAPER 15   12 MINS

During the evening of July, 8, number 88 Victoria Street, Grimley, was set on fire. The police are treating the fire as suspicious.

The only facts known at this stage are:

• Sarah Williams owns the house.
• The occupants had recently taken out insurance.
• A neighbour, Katie Forester, was known to dislike Miss Williams.
• Between July 8 and July 15, Mrs Forester was away on holiday in Spain
• No one died in the blaze.
• A Mrs Williams had been recorded buying petrol from a local petrol station on July 8.

A = TRUE B = FALSE C = IMPOSSIBLE TO SAY

1. Sarah Williams died in the blaze.
2. Katie Forester may have started the blaze.
3. Miss Williams was recorded buying petrol from a local petrol station on July 8.
4. Katie Forester lives at 87 Victoria Street.
5. Miss Williams may have started the blaze to benefit from an insurance claim.

TEST PAPER 16   12 MINS

A Police traffic unit pulled over a suspected drink driver because his driving was erratic. The driver said he had been to a house party and had only had one can of beer.

The only facts known at this stage are:

• The car was a five-door estate.
• The car had three occupants.
• Two of the occupants admitted having had consumed alcohol.
• James Culshaw was the driver.
• The driver failed the road side breath test.
• The party was less than one-mile from the location where Mr Culshaw was stopped.

A = TRUE B = FALSE C = IMPOSSIBLE TO SAY

1. Mr Culshaw told the Police he had not consumed any alcohol that night.
2. Mr Culshaw had more than one can of beer.
3. The passengers were also drunk.
4. Mr Culshaw was pulled over because he didn't have his lights on.
5. Mr Culshaw had a full car load.

TEST PAPER 17   12 MINS

Mr Rawlings lives on Sutcliffe Drive. On November 3, Mr Rawling had a firework put through the letterbox of his bungalow. This set the house on fire. Mr Rawlings was assisted out his house by his neighbours, Mr Hawkins and Mr Jenkins. Two fire appliances attended and it took 32-minutes to extinguish the flames. A teenager rang 999 to report the fire. Teenagers were seen loitering close to Mr Rawlings house.

The only facts known at this stage are:

• Mr Rawlings had recently been in court as a witness against a local teenager, Tyrone Mills.
• Mr Rawlings is elderly and finds it difficult to walk or climb stairs.
• Mr Rawlings has reported anti-social behaviour around his house to police.
• It took the fire service six- minutes to attend the call.
• Mr Rawlings lives on his own but does have family who visit.
• The firework was put through his door at 20:35.
• The teenager called the emergency services at 20:45.

A = TRUE B = FALSE C = IMPOSSIBLE TO SAY

1. The fire was extinguished between 21:20 and 21:30.
2. The firework was payback for Mr Rawlings going to court.
3. Mr Rawlings may have been upstairs when the fire started.
4. Mr Rawlings neighbours, Mrs Hawkins and Mrs Jenkins, helped him out his house.
5. It took one fire engine 32 minutes to extinguish the fire.

TEST PAPER 18   12 MINS

This morning at 6am Shepham Police raided a property with a warrant to search it for drugs. They found a selection of items commonly used to grow cannabis and a number of small cannabis plants. Police are still searching the property.

The latest reported facts are:

• The house is owned by Amanda Holder.
• She lives in the property with her partner, Michael Smith and his son, James Smith.
• Amanda and James do not get along.
• Michael works on an oil rig and has been away from home for two months.
• The drug growing equipment was found in James' room.
• All three have previous convictions for possessing drugs.

A = TRUE B = FALSE C = IMPOSSIBLE TO SAY

1. Amanda Holder has been convicted of producing drugs before.
2. The door of the house was damaged in the drug raid.
3. Michael may not be aware of the drugs.
4. James may have been growing the drugs to spite Amanda.
5. Michael may have planted the cannabis plants a month ago.

As part of a summer drink driving clampdown Doggington Police are stopping drivers randomly and asking them to provide voluntary breath samples.

The only facts known about the campaign so far are:

• On the first night 65 drivers agreed to provide samples.
• One of them was over the legal drink-drive limit.
• Sarah Newman had been drinking in the pub all day after splitting up with her partner.
• Police asked her to provide a sample after she hit a kerb while driving.
• She failed the roadside breath test and was taken into custody until she sobered up.
• The car she was driving belonged to her partner.

A = TRUE B = FALSE C = IMPOSSIBLE TO SAY

1. Sarah Newman was not insured to drive the car.
2. She damaged the wheel of the car when she drove it into the kerb.
3. Sarah Newman failed to provide a breath sample at the road side.
4. Sarah Newman was the only driver to fail the roadside breath test on the first night of the campaign.
5. She has been arrested for drink driving.

Jeff Bridges claims he has had his garden shed broken into. A crow bar was found in the garden and the door of the shed had been forced open using it. Mr Bridges claims that a lawn mower, a strimmer, a new spade and a garden fork have been stolen. He says that last week a group of young people graffitied the side wall of his house and he thinks they are to blame. The ringleader of the gang, Sam Smith has recently started a gardening company.

The latest reported facts are:

• Sam Smith had previous convictions for breaking and entering.
• Sam Smith has a variety of new gardening equipment for his company - including a spade the same as Mr Bridges.
• Mr Bridges spade was bought from popular high street shop B & P.
• Mr Bridges claims the items stolen were worth £400.
• Mr Bridges says Sam Smith has been harassing him.
• Sam Smith's dad fired Mr Bridges from his marketing company last month.

A = TRUE B = FALSE C = IMPOSSIBLE TO SAY

1. Mr Bridges had a grudge against Sam Smith.
2. The items stolen from Mr Bridges shed are worth more than £400.
3. Sam Smith may have stolen Mr Bridges spade.
4. The crow bar found in Mr Bridges garden was used to force open the shed.
5. Police may find Sam Smith's fingerprints at the scene.

RESULTS

Test Number	Question 1	Question 2	Question 3	Question 4	Question 5
1	A	B	C	C	B
2	B	A	C	C	C
3	C	B	A	C	B
4	B	B	C	C	C
5	C	A	A	B	C
6	A	C	C	C	C
7	B	C	C	A	A
8	A	A	C	C	B
9	C	B	C	B	C
10	A	A	B	A	C
11	A	C	B	B	B
12	B	C	A	A	B
13	A	C	C	A	C
14	A	B	C	C	B
15	B	A	B	C	A
16	B	C	C	B	B
17	A	C	B	B	B
18	C	C	A	A	B
19	C	C	B	A	C
20	C	C	A	A	A

Printed in Great Britain
by Amazon